BOOK 2

PHONICS AND LIFE SKILLS READING
FOR
Adult Literacy, ABE, and ESL Students

Turning Learners into Proficient Readers

Copyright ©2024 Coaching for Better Learning, LLC

All rights reserved.

CONTENTS

PREFACE FOR INSTRUCTORS 4

INTRODUCTION FOR LEARNERS 5

LESSON 1: SHORT VOWEL SOUNDS 6

LESSON 2: LONG VOWEL SOUNDS 11

LESSON 3: SPECIAL VOWEL SOUNDS 16

LESSON 4: VOWEL SOUNDS WITH R 22

LESSON 5: THE CONSONANT SOUNDS 28

LESSON 6: SPECIAL CONSONANT SOUNDS (GROUP 1) 35

LESSON 7: SPECIAL CONSONANT SOUNDS (GROUP 2) 42

LESSON 8: VOCABULARY AND SOUNDS 48

LESSON 9: READING ALOUD AND COMPREHENSION QUESTIONS 53

LESSON 10: STRATEGIES TO INCREASE YOUR VOCABULARY AND
IMPROVE YOUR READING SKILLS 70

ABOUT CBL 72

MORE TEXTBOOKS BY CBL 73

PREFACE FOR INSTRUCTORS

Dear Instructors,

Equip your adult literacy, ABE, and ESL students with the ultimate phonics resource that is designed to help them master the 44 sounds of English. This phonics and reading textbook offers a robust curriculum that includes reading activities, dictation exercises, and vocabulary building.

This book content is aligned with the English Language Proficiency Standards (ELPS) for Adult Education. It satisfies the expectations of the National Reporting System (NRS) and Workforce Innovation and Opportunity Act (WIOA), ensuring your ESL students are on the path to success.

Each lesson is carefully written to ensure students gain confidence and fluency by reading aloud, answering comprehension questions, and using vocabulary in context. With answer keys included, instructors can easily track progress and provide targeted support.

Starting with short vowel sounds and advancing through long vowel sounds, special vowel sounds, and various consonant sounds, this textbook provides a simple, comprehensive approach to phonics. The structured lessons, such as "Introducing the Short Vowel Sounds" and "Reading Aloud and Comprehension Questions," ensure that students consistently practice and reinforce their skills.

By practicing sounds and reading sentences and texts aloud, students will build a strong foundation in phonics, paving the way for improved reading skills. Indeed, this book is an essential tool that can help transform your classroom into a dynamic environment for phonics and reading mastery.

The CBL Team

INTRODUCTION FOR LEARNERS

Dear Students,

This phonics and reading textbook will help you master the 44 sounds of English. It presents engaging activities to build your reading, speaking, and vocabulary skills. Each lesson will guide you through different sounds and provide practice opportunities to ensure you gain confidence and fluency in reading.

By reading aloud, answering comprehension questions, and using new vocabulary in context, you'll improve your reading skills day by day.

In this textbook, you will find:

- Reading Activities: Enhance your reading skills through diverse and interesting texts.
- Dictation Activities: Practice listening and writing skills by completing dictation exercises.
- Vocabulary Building: Expand your vocabulary with targeted exercises and contextual applications.
- Answer Keys: Check your progress and understand your mistakes.

The lessons cover essential topics, such as:

- Short Vowel Sounds: Starting with the basics to build a strong foundation.
- Long Vowel Sounds: Progressing to more complex sounds.
- Special Sounds: Understanding sounds like "ar," "er," and "ire."
- Consonant Sounds: Mastering all the consonants in English.
- Special Consonant Sounds: Focusing on tricky sounds like "ch" and "sh."
- Vocabulary Exercises: Filling in blanks and reading sentences aloud to reinforce learning.
- Comprehension Questions: Reading texts aloud and answering questions to ensure understanding.

This book will help you develop a solid understanding of English sounds, which will greatly improve your reading, writing, and speaking abilities.

Enjoy your learning journey!

The CBL Team

LESSON 1

SHORT VOWEL SOUNDS

Objectives:
1. Students will identify and produce short vowel sounds.
2. Students will read short texts with short vowel sounds and answer comprehension questions correctly.

Exercise 1- Read aloud and repeat the letters and sounds below.

Vowel Sounds	Sound Symbols	Sample Words
Short A	/æ/	and, as, after, cat, bat
Short E	/ɛ/	pen, hen, lend, bed, red
Short I	/ɪ/	it, in, sit, bit, hit
Short O	/ɒ/	top, hop, not, pot, hot
Short U	/ʌ/	under, cup, cut, sun, run

Exercise 2- Read the following sentences aloud and <u>underline</u> the short vowel sounds.

1. The black bat flies fast.
2. The red pen is on the bed.
3. It is fun to run in the sun.
4. The top is on the hot pot.
5. The hen and the pen are in the den.

Exercise 3- Read the text aloud before answering the questions.

Tom has a cat and a dog. The cat likes to sit on the mat. The dog likes to hop and run. Tom feeds the cat and the dog every day. The cat and the dog are friends. They play together in the sun. Tom loves his pets very much. He takes good care of them. The cat's name is Sam and the dog's name is Max. They make Tom very happy.

Comprehension Questions:

1. What pets does Tom have?
   _____

2. Where does the cat like to sit?
   _____

3. What does the dog like to do?
   _____

4. What are the names of Tom's pets?
   _____

Exercise 4- Read the text aloud before answering the questions.

Ann likes to read books. She also writes about the books she reads. She has a red pen and a blue pen. Ann sits on her bed and reads at night. She likes to read about cats and dogs. Her friend Ben also likes to read. They often talk about their favorite books. Ann and Ben go to the library on weekends. They love to find new books to read. Reading makes Ann very happy.

Comprehension Questions:

1. What does Ann like to do?
   _____

2. What colors are Ann's pens?

   _____

3. When does Ann sit on her bed and read?

   _____

4. Where do Ann and Ben go on weekends?

   _____

Exercise 5- Read the text aloud before answering the questions.

> Jim likes to play in the park. He runs and jumps with his friends. The park has a big slide and a swing. Jim and his friends like to slide and swing. They also like to play tag. Jim's mom packs a snack for him. He eats the snack under a big tree. After playing, Jim is very tired. He goes home and takes a nap.

Comprehension Questions:

1. Where does Jim like to play?

   _____

2. What does Jim do with his friends?

   _____

3. What does Jim's mom pack for him?

   _____

4. What does Jim do after playing?

   _____

Exercise 6- Dictation # 1

Your teacher will read some words from the table in Exercise 1. Circle the words you hear.

1. hot, not, top, pot
2. bat, and, cat, after
3. cup, run, cut, under
4. pet, lend, bed, red
5. in, sit, bit, hit

Exercise 7- Dictation # 2

Your teacher will read some words from the table in Exercise 1. Write the words you hear.

_____   _____   _____   _____

_____   _____   _____   _____

Answer Keys

Exercise 2

1. The black bat flies fast.
2. The red pen is on the bed.
3. It is fun to run in the sun.
4. The top is on the hot pot.
5. The hen and the pen are in the den.

Exercise 3

1. Tom has a cat and a dog.
2. The cat likes to sit on the mat.
3. The dog likes to hop and run.
4. The cat's name is Sam and the dog's name is Max.

Exercise 4

1. Ann likes to read books.
2. Ann has a red pen and a blue pen.
3. Ann sits on her bed and reads at night.
4. Ann and Ben go to the library on weekends.

Exercise 5

1. Jim likes to play in the park.
2. Jim runs and jumps with his friends.
3. Jim's mom packs a snack for him.
4. Jim goes home and takes a nap.

REFLECTION ON LEARNING

Let's reflect on your progress.

1. What sounds did you learn and practice?

2. What sounds do you struggle with?

3. What strategies can you use to make more progress?

4. What do you want your instructor to know about your challenges?

LESSON 2

LONG VOWEL SOUNDS

Objectives:

1. Students will identify and produce long vowel sounds.
2. Students will read short texts with long vowel sounds and answer comprehension questions correctly.

Exercise 1- Read aloud and repeat the letters and sounds below.

Vowel Sound	Sound Symbol	Examples
Long A	/eɪ/	gate, take, cake, name, game
Long E	/iː/	he, sweet, see, tree, meet
Long I	/aɪ/	tie, lie, fight, bike, kite
Long O	/oʊ/	coat, toe, boat, nose, stone
Long U	/juː/	human, menu, use, cube, fuse
Long OO	/uː/	tool, droop, moon, food, pool

11

Exercise 2- Read the following sentences aloud and <u>underline</u> the long vowel sounds.

1. I will take the cake to the game.
2. The tree is tall and full of green leaves.
3. She will ride her bike to the park.
4. Nia tied her kite to the tree.
5. The puppy played with a huge cube.
6. He used a tool to fix the shelf.

Exercise 3- Read the text aloud before answering the questions.

Jane likes to bake cakes. She makes a big cake for every family event. Last week, she baked a chocolate cake for her cousin's birthday. Everyone loved the cake and asked for more. Jane enjoys trying new recipes. She also likes to take pictures of her cakes. Baking is Jane's favorite hobby. She hopes to open a bakery one day. Her family supports her dream. They believe she will be successful.

Comprehension Questions:

1. What does Jane like to do?
   _____

2. What did Jane bake for her cousin's birthday?
   _____

3. What does Jane hope to do one day?
   _____

4. What does Jane's family believe?
   _____

Exercise 4- Read the text aloud before answering the questions.

Mark enjoys going to the park. He rides his bike there every morning. The park is quiet and peaceful. Mark likes to sit under a tree and read. Sometimes, he brings a kite to fly. The fresh air makes him feel happy. Mark often meets his friends at the park. They play games and talk about their day. The park is Mark's favorite place to relax. He goes there whenever he can.

Comprehension Questions:

1. Where does Mark like to go?
   _____

2. What does Mark do under the tree?
   _____

3. What does Mark bring to the park sometimes?
   _____

4. Who does Mark often meet at the park?
   _____

Exercise 5- Read the text aloud before answering the questions.

Anna loves music. She listens to music every day. Her favorite instrument is the flute. Anna plays the flute in her school band. She practices for an hour each day. The music makes her feel calm and happy. Anna dreams of becoming a musician. She wants to travel and perform all over the world. Her parents encourage her to follow her passion. They believe in her talent.

Comprehension Questions:

1. What is Anna's favorite instrument?
   _____

2. Where does Anna play the flute?
   _____

3. How does music make Anna feel?
   _____

4. What is Anna's dream?
   _____

Exercise 6- Dictation # 1

Your teacher will read some words from the table in Exercise 1. Circle the words you hear.

1. take, name, cake, game
2. feet, see, sweet, tree

3. lie, bike, kite fight
4. toe, nose, boat, stone
5. menu, human, use, cube
6. pool, tool, food, moon

Exercise 7- Dictation # 2

Your teacher will read some words from the table in Exercise 1. Write the words you hear.

_____   _____   _____   _____

_____   _____   _____   _____

Answer Keys

Exercise 2

1. **I** will t**a**ke the c**a**ke to the g**a**me.
2. The tr**ee** is tall and full of gr**ee**n l**ea**ves.
3. Sh**e** will r**i**de her b**i**ke to the park.
4. Nia t**ie**d her k**i**te to the tr**ee**.
5. The puppy pl**ay**ed with a h**u**ge c**u**be.
6. H**e** **u**sed a t**oo**l to fix the shelf.

Exercise 3

1. Jane likes to bake cakes.
2. Jane baked a chocolate cake for her cousin's birthday.
3. Jane hopes to open a bakery one day.
4. They believe she will be successful.

Exercise 4

1. Mark likes to go to the park.
2. Mark reads under the tree.
3. Mark sometimes brings a kite to the park.
4. Mark often meets his friends at the park.

Exercise 5

1. Anna's favorite instrument is the flute.
2. Anna plays the flute in her school band.
3. Music makes Anna feel calm and happy.
4. Anna's dream is to become a musician and perform all over the world.

REFLECTION ON LEARNING

Let's reflect on your progress.

1. What sounds did you learn and practice?

2. What sounds do you struggle with?

3. What strategies can you use to make more progress?

4. What do you want your instructor to know about your challenges?

LESSON 3

SPECIAL VOWEL SOUNDS

Objectives:

1. Students will identify and produce special vowel sounds
2. Students will read short texts with special vowel sounds and answer comprehension questions correctly.

Exercise 1- Read aloud and repeat the letters and sounds below.

Sound	Sound Symbol	Examples
aw	/ɔ:/	paw, yawn, draw, straw
oi	/ɔɪ/	oil, boy, boil, choice, noise
ow	/aʊ/	owl, ouch, cow, now, brown
ow	/ō/	show, snow, throw, below
ey	/eɪ/	they, obey, convey, gray, pray

16

ew	/juː/ or /uː/	blew, new, chew, flew, grew
oo (short)	/ʊ/	cook, foot, good, hood
ai	/eɪ/	fail, train, maid, paint, aim
oa	/oʊ/	home, phone, coat, soap, toast
ei	/eɪ/	reign, weigh, neighbor, vein
ea	/iː/	seat, read, bead, team, dream
ea	/ɛ/	head, bread, health, pleasant
ie	/aɪ/	pie, tie, cry, slide
ie	/iː/	chief, field, belief, piece
oe	/oʊ/	toe, foe, goes, hoe, doe
ou	/aʊ/	cloud, shout, loud, found

Exercise 2- Read the following sentences aloud and underline the special vowel sounds.

1. The oil in the pan started to boil.
2. The owl sat on the brown cow.
3. They will obey the grey-haired man.
4. A few birds flew to the new nest.
5. He read the book while he cooked dinner.
6. The rain made the train tracks wet.
7. He found the coat that fell onto the road.
8. She weighed the eight apples.
9. The child painted his favorite toy.
10. The loud shout made the dog run out.

Exercise 3- Read the text aloud before answering the questions.

Ann likes to paint while it is raining. The sound of the rain is peaceful. Her favorite thing to paint is her toy boat floating on the water. She also paints an owl. Sometimes, she sees an owl on a tree branch. The owl hoots and flies away when it sees her. Ann also loves to read books about animals. She often finds a quiet place to sit and read. One day, she found a book about owls and read it cover to cover. She learned a lot about their habits.

Comprehension Questions:

1. What does Ann like to do when it is raining?
   _____

2. What is Ann's favorite thing to paint?
   _____

3. What does the owl do when it sees Ann?
   _____

4. What kind of books does Ann love to read?
   _____

Exercise 4- Read the text aloud before answering the questions.

Mark and Jane took a boat trip on the lake. They packed a lunchbox of toast, fruit, and juice. As they floated on the water, they saw a group of ducks. The ducks quacked loudly and swam close to the boat. Mark tried to catch a fish, but he had no luck. Jane read a book about sea creatures while they floated. They enjoyed the peaceful afternoon and the sounds of nature. When they returned to shore, they felt refreshed and happy.

Comprehension Questions:

1. Where did Mark and Jane go on their trip?
   _____

2. What did they pack for lunch?
   _____

3. What did Mark try to do?
   _____

4. What book did Jane read?

_____

Exercise 5- Read the text aloud before answering the questions.

Sam found a coin on the road while walking to school. He picked it up and put it in his pocket. At school, his teacher gave a lesson about the weather. She talked about how rain forms and why it is important. Sam listened carefully and took notes. During lunch, Sam showed his friends the coin he found. They were excited and asked if they could see it. After school, Sam used the coin to buy a snack. He was happy with his lucky find.

Comprehension Questions:

1. What did Sam find on the road?

_____

2. What was the lesson about at school?

_____

3. What did Sam do during lunch?

_____

4. What did Sam do after school?

_____

Exercise 6- Dictation # 1

Your teacher will read some words from the table in Exercise 1. Circle the words you hear.

1. ouch, cow, now, brown
2. new, chew, flew, grew
3. home, phone, coat, soap
4. cloud, shout, loud, found
5. reign, weigh, neighbor, vein
6. boy, boil, choice, noise

Exercise 7- Dictation # 2

Your teacher will read some words from the table in Exercise 1. Write the words you hear.

_____   _____   _____   _____

_____   _____   _____   _____

Answer Keys

Exercise 2

1. The **oi**l in the pan started to b**oi**l.
2. The **ow**l sat on the br**ow**n c**ow**.
3. Th**ey** will ob**ey** the gr**ey**-haired man.
4. A f**ew** birds fl**ew** to the n**ew** n**e**st.
5. He r**ea**d the b**oo**k wh**i**le he c**oo**ked dinner.
6. The r**ai**n m**a**de the tr**ai**n tracks w**e**t.
7. He f**ou**nd the c**oa**t that f**e**ll onto the r**oa**d.
8. She w**ei**ghed the **ei**ght apples.
9. The ch**i**ld p**ai**nted his f**a**vorite t**oy**.
10. The l**ou**d sh**ou**t m**a**de the dog run **ou**t.

Exercise 3

1. Ann likes to paint.
2. Ann's favorite thing to paint is her toy boat floating on the water.
3. The owl hoots and flies away when it sees Ann.
4. Ann loves to read books about animals.

Exercise 4

1. Mark and Jane went on a boat trip on the lake.
2. They packed toast, fruit, and juice for lunch.
3. Mark tried to catch a fish.
4. Jane read a book about sea creatures.

Exercise 5

1. Sam found a coin on the road.
2. The lesson at school was about the weather.
3. During lunch, Sam showed his friends the coin he found.
4. After school, Sam used the coin to buy a snack.

REFLECTION ON LEARNING

Let's reflect on your progress.

1. What sounds did you learn and practice?

2. What sounds do you struggle with?

3. What strategies can you use to make more progress?

4. What do you want your instructor to know about your challenges?

LESSON 4

VOWEL SOUNDS WITH R

Objectives:

1. Students will identify and produce vowel sounds with R.
2. Students will read short texts that include vowel sounds with R and answer comprehension questions accurately.

Exercise 1- Read aloud and repeat the letters and sounds below.

Letter	Sound Example	Examples
ar	/ɑr/	jar, scar, star, yard, farm
er	/ɜr/	germ, serve, term, clerk
or	/ɔr/	storm, sport, short, north
ur	/ɜr/	curl, hurt, curve, burglar
ire	/aɪər/	hire, admire, inspire, entire
are	/ɛər/	stare, prepare, scare, dare

Exercise 2- Read the following sentences aloud and underline the sounds with R.

1. The road has a sharp curve ahead.
2. The short hike led to a farm in the north.
3. He used a fork to eat the pork.
4. Be careful not to burn your hand in the fire.
5. She will hire someone to wire the house.
6. The entire family admired the beautiful star.

Exercise 3- Read the text aloud before answering the questions.

A Day on the Farm

Sara loves to visit her grandparents' farm. She helps them take care of the animals. The cows are in the barn, and the chickens roam freely. Sara's favorite animal is the big brown horse. She rides it every afternoon. After riding, she likes to sit under a tree and read. During her visits, her grandmother makes the best apple pie. They eat it together on the porch while watching the sunset. Sara feels very happy and relaxed on the farm.

Sara's grandfather tells her stories about the farm. He also talks about the days when he was young and how things have changed. Sara listens carefully and asks many questions. She learns a lot from him. They often go for walks around the farm. They talk about the plants and animals they see. Sara loves spending time with her grandparents. The farm is her favorite place to be. She always looks forward to her visits.

Comprehension Questions:

1. Where does Sara love to visit?

   _____

2. What is her favorite animal?

   _____

3. What does she do every afternoon?

   _____

4. What does her grandfather tell her stories about?

   _____

Exercise 4- Read the text aloud before answering the questions.

Mike's Busy Day

Mike works as a clerk in a big office. He sits at his desk and answers phone calls. His job is to help people with their questions. Mike likes to take short breaks to stretch his legs. During lunch, he eats with his friends. They talk about their day and share jokes. After work, Mike goes to the gym to exercise. He cares about staying healthy.

In the evening, Mike likes to relax at home. He watches his favorite TV shows and reads books. Sometimes, he goes out with friends. They go to the movies or have dinner together. Mike also likes to cook. He tries new recipes and shares them with his friends. On weekends, Mike goes hiking. He loves being in nature. Mike enjoys his job and his daily routine. He has a busy but fulfilling life.

Comprehension Questions:

1. Where does Mike work?

   _____

2. What does Mike do during lunch?

   _____

3. How does Mike stay healthy?

   _____

4. What does Mike do on weekends?

   _____

Exercise 5- Read the text aloud before answering the questions.

Exploring the Forest

Liam loves to explore the forest near his home. He takes his dog with him on long walks. They follow the path and look for interesting plants and animals. One day, they found a small cave hidden behind some bushes. Inside the cave, they saw strange drawings on the walls. Liam took pictures to show his family. They were excited and planned to visit the cave together. Liam loves discovering new places.

> On weekends, Liam goes to the forest with his friends. They have picnics and play games. Sometimes, they camp overnight. They sit around the fire and tell stories. Liam's friends enjoy exploring the forest as much as he does. They often find new trails to hike. Liam feels happy and free in the forest. He treasures these moments with his friends and dog.

Comprehension Questions:

1. Who does Liam take with him on walks?
   _____

2. What does Liam find behind the bushes?
   _____

3. What do Liam and his friends do when camping?
   _____

4. How does Liam feel in the forest?
   _____

Exercise 6- Dictation # 1

Your teacher will read some words from the table in Exercise 1. Circle the words you hear.

1. scar, star, yard, farm
2. germ, serve, term, clerk
3. storm, sport, short, north
4. curl, hurt, curve, burglar
5. hire, admire, inspire, entire
6. stare, prepare, scare, dare

Exercise 7- Dictation # 2

Your teacher will read some words from the table in Exercise 1. Write the words you hear.

_____ _____ _____ _____

_____ _____ _____ _____

Answer Keys

Exercise 2

1. The road has a sh<u>ar</u>p c<u>ur</u>ve ahead.
2. The sh<u>or</u>t hike led to a f<u>ar</u>m in the n<u>or</u>th.
3. He used a f<u>or</u>k to eat the p<u>or</u>k.
4. Be c<u>are</u>ful not to b<u>ur</u>n your hand in the f<u>ire</u>.
5. She will h<u>ire</u> someone to w<u>ire</u> the house.
6. The ent<u>ire</u> family adm<u>ire</u>d the beautiful st<u>ar</u>.

Exercise 3

1. Sara loves to visit her grandparents' farm.
2. Her favorite animal is the big brown horse.
3. She rides the horse every afternoon.
4. Her grandfather tells her stories about the farm.

Exercise 4

1. Mike works as a clerk in a big office.
2. Mike eats with his friends and they talk about their day and share jokes.
3. Mike goes to the gym to stay healthy.
4. Mike goes hiking on weekends.
5.

Exercise 5

1. Liam takes his dog with him on walks.
2. Liam finds a small cave hidden behind some bushes.
3. Liam and his friends sit around the fire and tell stories.
4. Liam feels happy and free in the forest.

REFLECTION ON LEARNING

Let's reflect on your progress.

1. What sounds did you learn and practice?

2. What sounds do you struggle with?

3. What strategies can you use to make more progress?

4. What do you want your instructor to know about your challenges?

LESSON 5

THE CONSONANT SOUNDS

Objectives:

1. Students will identify and produce the consonant sounds in words and sentences.
2. Students will read short texts that include the consonant sounds and accurately answer questions based on the texts.

Exercise 1- Read aloud and repeat the letters ad sounds below.

Letter	Sound Symbol	Examples
B	/b/	bat, ball, cabin, grab
K	/k/	kite, king, kiss, kid
D	/d/	doll, desk, sand, door
F	/f/	fish, fan, food, leaf
G	/g/	goat, game, gift, bag

H	/h/	hat, house, horse, behind
J	/dʒ/	jam, jug, jump, project
L	/l/	lamp, leg, leaf, lake
M	/m/	man, moon, milk, family
N	/n/	net, nap, nose, winter
P	/p/	pen, pig, campus, stop
R	/r/	rat, red, rope, parent
S	/s/	sea, soup, basic, bus
T	/t/	top, ten, water, cat
V	/v/	vest, vase, vote, level
W	/w/	web, win, wall, towel
X	/ks/	relax, next, fox, mix
Y	/j/	yes, yarn, may, yolk
Z	/z/	zoo, zero, zone, lazy

Exercise 2- Read the following sentences aloud and underline the consonant sounds.

1. The bat flew over the barn.
2. The king wore a gold crown.
3. The dog dug a hole in the yard.
4. The fish swam in the clear water.
5. The goat jumped over the fence.
6. The hat was too big for his head.

7. The jam was sweet and delicious.
8. The lamp lit up the dark room.
9. The man read a book by the lake.
10. The net caught the flying ball.
11. The pen rolled off the desk.
12. The rat ran across the road.
13. The sun shone brightly in the sky.
14. The top spun on the table.
15. The vest was made of soft wool.
16. The web was spun by a spider.
17. The yarn was tangled in a knot.
18. The zoo had many exotic animals.

Exercise 3- Read the text aloud before answering the questions.

A Day at the Zoo

Liam and his sister went to the zoo on a sunny day. They saw a big lion roaring loudly. The monkeys were swinging from the trees. Liam loved watching the elephants play in the water. His sister liked the colorful birds in the aviary. They ate lunch by the lake and fed the ducks. The zookeeper gave them a tour of the reptile house. They saw snakes and lizards up close.

Liam's favorite animal was the giraffe. He watched it eat leaves from the tall trees. His sister's favorite was the panda, which was eating bamboo. They took many pictures to remember the day. Liam and his sister learned a lot about different animals. It was an exciting day for both of them. They talked about the animals all the way home. They decided to visit the zoo again soon. The zoo became their favorite place to visit.

Comprehension Questions:

1. Where did Liam and his sister go on a sunny day?

   _____

2. What was Liam's favorite animal?

   _____

3. What did Liam's sister like in the aviary?

   _____

4. What did they do by the lake?

   _____

Exercise 4- Read the text aloud before answering the questions.

The School Science Fair

Jenny was excited about the school science fair. She worked hard on her project about volcanoes. She made a model that could erupt with baking soda and vinegar. Jenny's classmates were impressed by her demonstration. She explained how real volcanoes work. The judges asked her many questions about her project. Jenny was nervous but answered them confidently. Her teacher praised her for her hard work. At the end of the day, Jenny won first prize.

Jenny's parents were very proud of her. They took her out for ice cream to celebrate. Jenny was happy and thanked her parents for their support. She decided she wanted to be a scientist when she grew up. Her teacher encouraged her to keep learning and exploring. Jenny looked forward to the next science fair. She was already thinking of new ideas for her project.

Comprehension Questions:

1. What was Jenny's project about?

   _____

2. How did Jenny make her model erupt?

   _____

3. What did Jenny win at the science fair?

   _____

4. How did Jenny's parents celebrate her success?

   _____

Exercise 5- Read the text aloud before answering the questions.

A Walk in the Park

Tom and his friend, Sam, went for a walk in the park. They saw children playing on the swings and slides. Tom and Sam played soccer on the grass. They ran and kicked the ball to each other. After a while, they sat under a tree to rest. Tom took out a book and started to read. Sam looked for birds in the branches. They enjoyed the peaceful atmosphere of the park. It was a perfect day to be outside.

> Tom and Sam also found a small pond in the park. They watched the fish swim and the ducks paddle on the water. Tom threw some breadcrumbs to the ducks. Sam took pictures of the fish with his camera. They walked around the pond and talked about their plans for the weekend. Tom wanted to go hiking, and Sam wanted to visit his grandparents. They both agreed to meet at the park again soon.

Comprehension Questions:

1. Where did Tom and Sam go for a walk?
   _____

2. What did Tom and Sam do on the grass?
   _____

3. What did Sam do with his camera?
   _____

4. What did Tom and Sam plan to do the following weekend?
   _____

Exercise 6- Dictation # 1

Your teacher will read some words from the table in Exercise 1. Circle the words you hear.

1. fish, fan, food, leaf
2. man, moon, milk, family
3. doll, desk, sand, door
4. sea, soup, basic, bus
5. relax, next, fox, mix
6. jam, jug, jump, project

Exercise 7- Dictation # 2

Your teacher will read some words from the table in Exercise 1. Write the words you hear.

_____ _____ _____ _____

_____ _____ _____ _____

Answer Keys

Exercise 2

1. The <u>b</u>at <u>fl</u>ew <u>ov</u>er the <u>b</u>arn.
2. The <u>k</u>ing <u>w</u>ore a <u>g</u>old <u>cr</u>own.
3. The <u>d</u>og <u>d</u>ug a <u>h</u>ole in the <u>y</u>ard.
4. The <u>f</u>ish <u>sw</u>am <u>i</u>n the <u>c</u>lear <u>w</u>ater.
5. The <u>g</u>oat <u>j</u>umped <u>o</u>ver the <u>f</u>ence.
6. The <u>h</u>at <u>w</u>as <u>t</u>oo <u>b</u>ig <u>f</u>or <u>h</u>is <u>h</u>ead.
7. The <u>j</u>am <u>w</u>as <u>sw</u>eet <u>and</u> <u>d</u>elicious.
8. The <u>l</u>amp <u>l</u>it up the <u>d</u>ark <u>r</u>oom.
9. The <u>m</u>an <u>r</u>ead a <u>b</u>ook <u>by</u> the <u>l</u>ake.
10. The <u>n</u>et <u>c</u>aught the <u>fl</u>ying <u>b</u>all.
11. The <u>p</u>en <u>r</u>olled <u>off</u> the <u>d</u>esk.
12. The <u>r</u>at <u>r</u>an <u>a</u>cross the <u>r</u>oad.
13. The <u>s</u>un sho<u>n</u>e <u>br</u>ightly <u>i</u>n the <u>sk</u>y.
14. The <u>t</u>op <u>sp</u>un <u>o</u>n the <u>t</u>able.
15. The <u>v</u>est <u>w</u>as <u>m</u>ade <u>o</u>f <u>s</u>oft <u>w</u>ool.
16. The <u>w</u>eb <u>w</u>as <u>sp</u>un <u>by</u> a <u>sp</u>ider.
17. The <u>y</u>arn <u>w</u>as <u>t</u>angled <u>in</u> a <u>k</u>not.
18. The <u>z</u>oo <u>h</u>ad <u>m</u>any <u>ex</u>otic <u>a</u>nimals.

Exercise 3

1. Liam and his sister went to the zoo on a sunny day.
2. Liam's favorite animal was the giraffe.
3. Liam's sister liked the colorful birds in the aviary.
4. They ate lunch by the lake and fed the ducks.

Exercise 4

1. Jenny's project was about volcanoes.
2. Jenny made her model erupt with baking soda and vinegar.
3. Jenny won first prize at the science fair.
4. Jenny's parents took her out for ice cream to celebrate.

Exercise 5

1. Tom and Sam went for a walk in the park.
2. Tom and Sam played soccer on the grass.
3. Sam took pictures of the fish with his camera.
4. Tom wanted to go hiking, and Sam wanted to visit his grandparents.

REFLECTION ON LEARNING

Let's reflect on your progress.

1. What sounds did you learn and practice?

2. What sounds do you struggle with?

3. What strategies can you use to make more progress?

4. What do you want your instructor to know about your challenges?

LESSON 6

SPECIAL CONSONANT SOUNDS (GROUP 1)

Objectives:

1. Students will identify and produce special consonant sounds (two or three consonants combine their sounds) in words and sentences.
2. Students will read short texts that include these consonant sounds and answer questions based on the texts.

Exercise 1- Read aloud and repeat the letters ad sounds below.

Letter	Sound Symbol	Examples
bl	/bl/	**bl**ack, **bl**anket, **bl**ink, **bl**oom, **bl**ast
br	/br/	**br**ead, **br**idge, **br**ush, **br**ave, **br**ick
cl	/kl/	**cl**imb, **cl**ock, **cl**own, **cl**ip, **cl**ick
cr	/kr/	**cr**own, **cr**ib, **cr**ash, **cr**eep, **cr**isp
dr	/dr/	**dr**ink, **dr**ive, **dr**op, **dr**um, **dr**eam
fl	/fl/	**fl**ower, **fl**oor, **fl**ame, **fl**ash, **fl**ock

fr	/fr/	frog, fruit, frame, frost, free
gl	/gl/	glow, globe, glide, glitter, glance
gr	/gr/	green, grass, grow, grape, grill
pl	/pl/	plant, plate, plug, plum, plan
pr	/pr/	print, price, press, proud, prize
sc	/sk/	scare, scold, scam, scatter, scoop
scr	/skr/	scrub, scrap, scream, scrub, scratch
sk	/sk/	skip, skin, skill, skull, sketch
sl	/sl/	sleep, slide, slim, slow, slipper
sm	/sm/	smart, smile, smell, smoke, small
sp	/sp/	speak, spin, splash, spoon, spider
spl	/spl/	splatter, splash, split, splurge, splendor
spr	/spr/	spring, spread, sprinkle, sprint, spray
squ	/skw/	square, squeal, squeeze, squirm, squat
st	/st/	star, storm, stick, stone, start
str	/str/	street, string, strong, strip, stress
sw	/sw/	swim, sweep, swing, switch, swell
tr	/tr/	train, truck, track, trail, trust
tw	/tw/	twist, twelve, twine, twitch, tweak

Exercise 2- Read the following sentences aloud and <u>underline</u> the special consonant sounds.

1. The blue bird flew over the black fence.
2. Please close the door and turn off the light.
3. The flowers bloom in the spring and glow in the sun.
4. The brave soldier crossed the bridge at dawn.
5. The clown climbed the tall tree to get the crown.
6. The frog jumped from the green grass into the pond.
7. The truck drove down the rocky trail.
8. The spider spun a web in the corner of the window.
9. The street was wet from the storm last night.
10. The sweet smell of the flowers filled the air.

Exercise 3- Read the text aloud before answering the questions.

A Trip to the Farm

Tom and his friends took a trip to the farm. They saw black cows grazing in the green fields. The farmer showed them how to plant seeds in the ground. They watched the chickens cluck and peck at the grain. The kids climbed up into the hayloft and played hide and seek. Tom found a small brown frog near the pond. They also saw a big red tractor plowing the field. The farmer let them ride on the tractor.

For lunch, they drank fresh milk from the cows and ate homemade bread. The farmer's wife also made them sweet lemonade. After, they helped the farmer gather eggs from the chicken coop. Tom and his friends then took a walk to the apple orchard. They picked apples and tasted the fresh fruit. As the sun began to set, they said goodbye to the farmer and his wife. They promised to visit again soon. The trip was full of fun and learning. It was a great day on the farm.

Comprehension Questions:

1. What animals did Tom and his friends see on the farm?

   _____

2. What did the kids do in the hayloft?

   _____

3. What did they drink with their lunch?

   _____

4. Where did they go to pick apples?

_____

Exercise 4- Read the text aloud before answering the questions.

The School Field Trip

Jenny's class went on a field trip to the science museum. They saw many amazing exhibits, including a giant dinosaur skeleton. Jenny and her friends took notes and drew pictures of the fossils. They learned how volcanoes erupt and saw a model volcano. The guide also showed them how to make slime, and they got to take some home. Jenny was excited to visit the planetarium and see the stars after.

In the afternoon, they visited the butterfly garden. The butterflies were bright and colorful. Jenny saw one land on a flower and took a picture. They walked through the garden and saw many types of plants. After the garden, they went to the gift shop. Jenny bought a blue bracelet and a book about space. The bus ride back to school was filled with chatter about their favorite parts of the trip. It was an educational and fun day.

Comprehension Questions:

1. Where did Jenny's class go for their field trip?

_____

2. What did Jenny and her friends do with the fossils?

_____

3. What did they see in the planetarium?

_____

4. What did Jenny buy at the gift shop?

_____

Exercise 5- Read the text aloud before answering the questions.

A Day at the Lake

Sam and his family spent the day at the lake. They spread a blanket on the grass and set up a picnic table. Sam and his brother built a small dam with rocks and sticks. They collected pebbles and smooth stones along the shore. Sam's sister flew a kite that soared high in the sky. The water lapped gently against the shore, and the birds chirped overhead.

> In the afternoon, they had a picnic with sandwiches and fruit. Sam swam in the lake and played frisbee with his dad. They found a small cove filled with tadpoles and small fish. Sam's mom took pictures of them playing. As the sun set, they gathered their things and headed home. It was a perfect day at the lake, and they all felt happy and relaxed.

Comprehension Questions:

1. What did Sam and his brother build on the lake?

_____

2. What did they collect along the shore?

_____

3. What did Sam's sister do at the lake?

_____

4. What did they find in the cove?

_____

Exercise 6- Dictation # 1

Your teacher will read some words from the table in Exercise 1. Circle the words you hear.

1. bread, bridge, brush, brave
2. crown, crib, crash, creep, crisp
3. scold, scam, scatter, scoop
4. skip, skin, skull, sketch
5. speak, spin, splash, spoon
6. train, truck, track, trail, trust

Exercise 7- Dictation # 2

Your teacher will read some words from the table in Exercise 1. Write the words you hear.

_____   _____   _____   _____

_____   _____   _____   _____

Answer Keys

Exercise 2

1. The **bl**ue bird **fl**ew over the **bl**ack fence.
2. **Pl**ease **cl**ose the door and turn off the light.
3. The **fl**owers **bl**oom in the **spr**ing and **gl**ow in the sun.
4. The **br**ave soldier **cr**ossed the **br**idge at dawn.
5. The **cl**own **cl**imbed the tall tree to get the **cr**own.
6. The **fr**og jumped **fr**om the **gr**een **gr**ass into the pond.
7. The **tr**uck **dr**ove down the rocky **tr**ail.
8. The **sp**ider **sp**un a web in the corner of the window.
9. The **str**eet was wet **fr**om the **st**orm last night.
10. The **sw**eet **sm**ell of the **fl**owers filled the air.

Exercise 3

1. They saw black cows, chickens, and a brown frog.
2. They played hide and seek in the hayloft.
3. They drank fresh milk and lemonade.
4. They went to the apple orchard to pick apples.

Exercise 4

1. They went to the science museum.
2. They took notes and drew pictures of the fossils.
3. They saw the stars in the planetarium.
4. Jenny bought a blue bracelet and a book about space.

Exercise 5

1. They built a small dam with rocks and sticks
2. They collected pebbles and smooth stones along the shore.
3. She flew the kite that soared high in the sky.
4. They found tadpoles and small fish in the cove.

REFLECTION ON LEARNING

Let's reflect on your progress.

1. What sounds did you learn and practice?

2. What sounds do you struggle with?

3. What strategies can you use to make more progress?

4. What do you want your instructor to know about your challenges?

LESSON 7

SPECIAL CONSONANT SOUNDS (GROUP 2)

Objectives:

1. Students will identify and produce special consonant sounds (two or three consonants make a new sound) in words and sentences.
2. Students will read short texts that include these consonant sounds and answer questions based on the texts.

Exercise 1- Read aloud and repeat the letters and sounds below.

Sound	Sound Symbol	Sample Words
ch	/tʃ/	child, chase, cheese, chair, rich
sh	/ʃ/	bush, shirt, share, shoe, wish
th	/θ/	think, teeth, thirsty, path, mouth
th	/ð/	though, gather, together, other, them
wh	/w/	white, what, why, where, whale

gn	/n/	assi**gn**, forei**gn**, si**gn**, ali**gn**, **gn**arl
kn	/n/	**kn**ead, **kn**owledge, **kn**ee, **kn**ot, **kn**it
gh	/f/	lau**gh**ter, tou**gh**, enou**gh**, rou**gh**, trou**gh**
ph	/f/	tro**ph**y, gra**ph**, ele**ph**ant, al**ph**abet

Exercise 2- Read the following sentences aloud and <u>underline</u> the special consonant sounds listed in Exercise 1.

1. The cheese on the table is rich and creamy.
2. She will shop for shoes and wish for a good sale.
3. The thin man walked on the path by the river.
4. This is the book that belongs to them.
5. When will we see the white whale?
6. The gnome signaled to the gnat in the garden.
7. The knight knew how to knit a scarf.
8. Their laughter echoed through the hall.
9. The phone rang with a loud tone.
10. The dentist reminded me to brush my teeth every day.

Exercise 3- Read the text aloud before answering the questions.

A Visit to the Aquarium

Chloe and her family visited an aquarium during the weekend. They saw colorful fish and dolphins in the tanks. The visitors read the signs to learn how to identify different sea creatures. Chloe's favorite exhibit was the shark tunnel. This was part of the aquarium's special attractions. The guide showed them how to touch starfish in the petting tank. Chloe also spotted a seahorse hiding among the rocks.

After lunch, they took a walk along a path that led to a high observation deck. From the top, they could see the whole aquarium. Chloe noticed a sign that pointed to a cave. Inside, they found old diving equipment and a knight's armor. Chloe was excited about the adventure. Her father took a photo of her standing next to the armor. The trip to the aquarium was educational and fun.

Comprehension Questions:

1. What was Chloe's favorite exhibit at the aquarium?

   _____

2. How did visitors learn to identify different sea creatures?

   _____

3. What did Chloe find among the rocks?

   _____

4. What did they find inside the cave?

   _____

Exercise 4- Read the text aloud before answering the questions.

The School Play

Nathan was excited about the school play. He had the role of a knight who had to rescue a princess. Nathan practiced his lines every day. His mother helped him make a costume with a shining helmet and a large shield. On the day of the play, the school hall was filled with parents and students. Nathan was nervous but remembered all his lines. His best friend played the role of a gnome who helped him on his quest.

The play was a big success, and everyone clapped loudly. After the play, Nathan's teacher praised him for his performance. His friends congratulated him and took pictures together. Nathan felt proud and happy. He knew that all the practice had paid off. The play ended with a grand feast, and Nathan sat at the table with his friends. It was a night he would always remember.

Comprehension Questions:

1. What role did Nathan play in the school play?

   _____

2. Who helped Nathan make his costume?

   _____

3. What was Nathan's best friend's role in the play?

   _____

4. How did Nathan feel after the play?

_____

Exercise 5- Read the text aloud before answering the questions.

A Day at the Beach

Rachel and her family spent a day at the beach. The weather was perfect, and the sky was clear. Rachel brought a picnic basket with sandwiches, fruit, and snacks. They found a spot near the water and spread out their blanket. Rachel's brother brought a beach ball, and they took turns tossing it to each other. The waves were gentle, and they enjoyed swimming in the cool water.

In the afternoon, they built a sandcastle with a moat around it. Rachel collected seashells and found a large, shiny one. She showed it to her mother, who said it looked like a rare find. They watched the sunset and packed up their things. As they were leaving, Rachel saw a sign that read, "Keep the Beach Clean." She picked up some trash and threw it away. It was a wonderful day. Although she was tired, she felt happy.

Comprehension Questions:

1. What did Rachel bring in the picnic basket?

_____

2. What did Rachel's brother bring to the beach?

_____

3. What did Rachel find on the beach?

_____

4. What did Rachel read on the sign as they were leaving?

_____

Exercise 6- Dictation # 1

Your teacher will read some words from the table in Exercise 1. Circle the words you hear.

1. child, chase, cheese, chair,
2. bush, shirt, share, shoe
3. think, teeth, thirsty, path
4. what, why, where, whale
5. knead, knowledge, knee, knot
6. laughter, tough, enough, rough

Exercise 7- Dictation # 2

Your teacher will read some words from the table in Exercise 1. Write the words you hear.

_____   _____   _____   _____

_____   _____   _____   _____

Answer Keys

Exercise 2

1. **Th**e **ch**eese on **th**e table is ri**ch** and creamy.
2. **Sh**e will **sh**op for **sh**oes and wi**sh** for a good sale.
3. **Th**e **th**in man walked on **th**e **p**a**th** by **th**e river.
4. **Th**is is **th**e book **th**at belongs to **th**em.
5. **Wh**en will we see the **wh**ite **wh**ale?
6. **Th**e **gn**ome signaled to **th**e **gn**at in **th**e garden.
7. **Th**e **kn**ight **kn**ew how to **kn**it a scarf.
8. **Th**eir lau**gh**ter echoed **th**rough **th**e hall.
9. **Th**e **ph**one rang wi**th** a loud tone.
10. **Th**e dentist reminded me to bru**sh** my tee**th** every day.

Exercise 3

1. Chloe's favorite exhibit was the shark tunnel.
2. The visitors read the signs.
3. Chloe found a seahorse among the rocks.
4. They found old diving equipment and a knight's armor inside the cave.

Exercise 4

1. Nathan played the role of a knight in the school play.
2. His mother helped him make his costume.
3. His best friend played the role of a gnome in the play.
4. He felt proud and happy after the play.

Exercise 5

1. Rachel brought a picnic basket with sandwiches, fruit, and snacks.
2. Rachel's brother brought a beach ball.
3. Rachel found a large, shiny seashell.
4. The sign said, "Keep the Beach Clean."

REFLECTION ON LEARNING

Let's reflect on your progress.

1. What sounds did you learn and practice?

2. What sounds do you struggle with?

3. What strategies can you use to make more progress?

4. What do you want your instructor to know about your challenges?

LESSON 8

VOCABULARY AND SOUNDS

Objectives:

1. Students will identify and use sounds to complete common words in sentences.
2. Students will practice reading sentences aloud to improve their pronunciation and increase their awareness of sounds in English.

Exercise 1- Family: Fill in the blanks with the correct letters or sounds (*a, e, i, o,* or *u*). Then, read each sentence aloud.

1. My br____ther is older than me by f____ve years.
2. Our family has a big d____nner every S____nday.
3. My mother loves to b____ke cookies.
4. We play g____mes with my ____ncle in the garden.
5. My s____ster is good at drawing and creates lovely sk____tches.
6. My father takes us to the park during the s____mmer.
7. Our grandpar____nts vis____t us during the holidays.

Exercise 2- Community Resources: Fill in the blanks with the correct letters or sounds (*ea, ar, ou, oo, ire,* or *i*). Then, read each sentence aloud.

1. The libr____y has many books to r____d.
2. We go to the p____k to play and relax.
3. The clinic is open for h____lth check-ups.

4. Our sch____l has a new playground.
5. The pol____ce station is near our h____se.
6. We can get fresh vegetables at the m____ket.
7. The f____ station is ready for emergencies.

Exercise 3- Workplace: Fill in the blanks with the correct letters or sounds (*ee, ea, ow, er, or, oo,* or *ar*). Then, read each sentence aloud.

1. The manager is in ch____ge of the t____m.
2. We have a m____ting every Monday m____ning.
3. The office is located downt____n.
4. I use a comput____ to complete my tasks.
5. The cafeteria s____ves lunch to employ____s.
6. We need to submit our rep____ts by Friday.
7. The conference r____m is on the second floor.

Exercise 4- Weather: Fill in the blanks with the correct letters or sounds (*ai, ow, er, or, ou, ea,* or *ar*). Then read each sentence aloud.

1. The cl____ds are blocking the sun today.
2. The r____n started in the aft____noon.
3. We expect sn____ in the evening.
4. The wind is bl____ing very strongly today.
5. The temp____ature is dropping fast.
6. The w____ther f____ecast says it will be cloudy tomorrow.
7. We saw a beautiful r____nbow after the st____m.

Exercise 5- Transportation: Fill in the blanks with the correct letters or sounds (*c, t, n, v, l, p,* or *s*). Then read each sentence aloud.

1. I take the bu____ to school every day.
2. The trai____ station is very busy in the mornings.
3. We need to put fue____ in the car before going on the tri____.
4. The bicy____le is a good way to exercise.
5. The airpla____e took off on time.
6. He likes to dri____e fast cars.
7. The boa____ sails on the lake.

Exercise 6- Shopping: Fill in the blanks with the correct letters or sounds (*ur, er, c, s, ie, ou, p, ei,* or *th*). Then read each sentence aloud.

1. The ___tore has a sale on clo___es.
2. I need to p___chase some groceries for dinner.
3. The cashi___ gave me my rec___pt.
4. We can find a var___ty of items in the mall.
5. She used a ___oupon to get a disc___nt.
6. The ___rice of this jacket is too high.
7. I prefer to sho___ online.

Exercise 7- Financial Literacy: Fill in the blanks with the correct letters or sounds (*cr, pl, st, tr, oa, br, sp,* or *cl*). Then, read each sentence aloud.

1. I opened an account last week at that bank ___anch.
2. We budget our money so we do not ___end too much.
3. She reviewed her bank ___atement carefully.
4. The l___n has a low interest rate.
5. We should invest in a good retirement ___an.
6. The bank ___lerk helped Carlos ___ansfer funds to his account.
7. The ___edit card can be used anywhere.

Exercise 8- Health Care Services: Fill in the blanks with the correct letters or sounds (*wh, ch, th, gh, er, ur,* or *ph*). Then, read each sentence aloud.

1. The doctor ___ecked my blood pressure.
2. The patient pointed to ___ere the pain was located.
3. The ___erapist showed me ex___cises to help me.
4. I bought my medicine at the ___armacy.
5. The n___se updated the patient's ___art.
6. Liam had to whisper due to a sore ___roat.
7. Recovery after s___gery can be tou___ and painful.

Answer Keys

Exercise 1- Family

1. brother, five
2. dinner, Sunday
3. bake
4. games, uncle
5. sister, sketches
6. summer
7. grandparents, visit

Exercise 2- Community Resources

1. library, read
2. park
3. health
4. school
5. police, house
6. market
7. fire

Exercise 3- Workplace

1. charge, team
2. meeting, morning
3. downtown
4. computer
5. serves, employees
6. reports
7. room

Exercise 4- Weather

1. clouds
2. rain, afternoon
3. snow
4. blowing
5. temperature
6. weather, forecast
7. rainbow, storm

Exercise 5- Transportation

1. bus
2. train
3. fuel, trip
4. bicycle
5. airplane
6. drive
7. boat

Exercise 6- Shopping

1. store, clothes
2. purchase
3. cashier, receipt
4. variety
5. coupon, discount
6. price
7. shop

Exercise 7- Financial Literacy

1. branch
2. spend
3. statement
4. loan
5. plan
6. clerk, transfer
7. credit

Exercise 8- Health Care Services

1. checked
2. where
3. therapist, exercises
4. pharmacy
5. nurse, chart
6. throat
7. surgery, tough

REFLECTION ON LEARNING

Let's reflect on your progress.

1. What sounds did you learn and practice?

2. What sounds do you struggle with?

3. What strategies can you use to make more progress?

4. What do you want your instructor to know about your challenges?

LESSON 9

READING ALOUD AND COMPREHENSION QUESTIONS

Objectives:

1. Students will read aloud various texts on practical life skills.
2. Students will answer comprehension questions based on these texts.

Exercise 1- Read the text aloud before answering the questions.

Workplace Safety Procedures

Workplace safety is essential to prevent accidents and injuries. Employees must follow safety guidelines, such as wearing protective gear. Helmets, gloves, and safety glasses are all important. Fire drills are conducted monthly to ensure everyone knows the evacuation routes. It is crucial to report any hazards immediately. Clear communication is key to maintaining a safe environment. Safety signs and labels should be visible. Regular maintenance of equipment prevents malfunctions. These tools and machinery must be used as instructed.

In case of an emergency, employees should know the location of fire extinguishers and first aid kits. Proper lifting techniques help prevent back injuries while wearing proper footwear can prevent slips and falls. It is also important to take breaks to avoid fatigue. Emergency exits should be accessible at all times. Employees should participate in safety audits. Regular training sessions help them stay updated on safety procedures. No one should ignore safety protocols. A culture of safety benefits everyone.

Comprehension Questions:

1. What are three types of protective gear mentioned?

_____

2. How often are fire drills conducted?

_____

3. Why is clear communication important in the workplace?

_____

4. What should employees know in case of an emergency?

_____

Exercise 2- Read the text aloud before answering the questions.

Types of Transportation

There are various types of transportation available for commuting. Cars are the most common mode of transportation. Buses provide an affordable option for many people. Trains are efficient for long-distance travel. Bicycles are eco-friendly and promote fitness. Airplanes are used for international travel. Boats and ferries are common in regions with many waterways. Walking is the simplest way to move from one place to another and it is good for the body's health. Each type of transportation has its own advantages and disadvantages.

Public transportation reduces traffic congestion and pollution. It is also cost-effective. However, it may not always be convenient. Private transportation offers flexibility and comfort. But it can be expensive due to fuel and maintenance costs. Carpooling is a good alternative to reduce expenses and environmental impact. Electric vehicles are becoming more popular as a sustainable option. Innovations in transportation technology continue to evolve, providing more choices for commuters.

Comprehension Questions:

1. What are three advantages of public transportation?

2. Name two types of eco-friendly transportation mentioned.

3. Why might private transportation be considered expensive?

4. What are two benefits of carpooling?

Exercise 3- Read the text aloud before answering the questions.

Managing a House Budget

Effective budgeting involves planning for both short-term and long-term expenses. Managing a household budget is crucial for financial stability. Start by listing all sources of income. Next, track your expenses, including bills and groceries. Identify areas where you can cut costs. Set aside a portion of your income to save for emergencies and future goals. Use budgeting tools or apps to keep track of your finances. Avoid unnecessary purchases to stay within your budget. Review your budget regularly to adjust your expenses. Prioritize paying off debts to reduce financial stress.

Meal planning can help reduce grocery costs. Consider energy-efficient appliances to lower utility bills. Use public transportation or carpool to save on fuel. Look for discounts and coupons when shopping. It's important to involve the entire family in budgeting decisions. Teach children the value of money and saving. A well-managed budget leads to financial security.

Comprehension Questions:

1. What is the first step in managing a household budget?

_____

2. Why is it important to set aside a portion of income for savings?

_____

3. How can meal planning help with budgeting?

_____

4. Why should the entire family be involved in budgeting decisions?

_____

5. What is a benefit of using energy-efficient appliances?

_____

Exercise 4- Read the text aloud before answering the questions.

Elections in the US

Elections in the United States are held to choose leaders and representatives. The process begins with primary elections, where candidates are selected. The general election follows, determining the final winners. Voters cast ballots to select their preferred candidates. The Electoral College plays a crucial role in presidential elections. Citizens must be registered to vote. Voting can take place in person or by mail. It is important to stay informed about candidates and issues.

The democratic process ensures that citizens have a voice in government. Elections are held at local, state, and national levels. Campaigns provide information about candidates' platforms. Debates allow candidates to present their views. Polling places are set up in communities for easy access. Election results are announced after all votes are counted. The peaceful transfer of power is a hallmark of democracy. Active participation in elections is a civic duty. Every vote counts.

Comprehension Questions:

1. What does the process of elections begin with?

   _____

2. Why is voter registration important?

   _____

3. What are the three levels at which elections are held?

   _____

4. What are two ways citizens can vote?

   _____

5. What is a hallmark of democracy mentioned in the text?

   _____

Exercise 5- Read the text aloud before answering the questions.

Voting in the US

Voting is a fundamental right in the United States. Citizens over the age of 18 are eligible to vote. It is important to register to vote before the election. Voter registration can be done online or in person. On Election Day, voters go to polling places to cast their ballots. Some states allow early voting to accommodate schedules. Absentee voting is available for those unable to vote in person. Each state has its own voting laws and procedures.

Voting ensures that citizens have a say in government decisions. It is important to research candidates and issues before voting. Campaigns provide information through advertisements and debates. Voters should check their polling place and voting hours. Identification may be required to vote. Election officials are available to assist voters at polling places. The results are announced after all votes are counted. Participation in elections strengthens democracy. Every vote makes a difference.

Comprehension Questions:

1. Who is eligible to vote in the United States?

___

2. What are two ways to register to vote?

___

3. How do campaigns provide information?

___

4. What may be required to vote at polling places?

___

5. What strengthens democracy according to the text?

___

Exercise 6- Read the text aloud before answering the questions.

Looking for Jobs

Finding a job requires preparation and persistence. Start by updating your resume with relevant experience. Write a compelling cover letter tailored to each job. Search for job openings online and in newspapers. Networking can help you learn about job opportunities. Attend job fairs to meet potential employers. Prepare for interviews by practicing common questions. Dress professionally and arrive on time. Follow up with a thank-you note after interviews.

Job search tools and resources can assist you in finding employment. Use job search websites to find openings in your field. Sign up for job alerts to receive notifications of new postings. Join professional organizations to connect with industry professionals. Take advantage of career counseling services. Improve your skills through training and education. Volunteering can provide valuable experience. Stay positive and persistent in your job search. Securing a job takes time and effort.

Comprehension Questions:

1. What should you update before starting a job search?

___

2. Why is networking important in a job search?

___

3. How can you prepare for job interviews?

___

4. What should you do after an interview?

___

5. Name two job search tools mentioned in the text.

___

Exercise 7- Read the text aloud before answering the questions.

Income and Sales Taxes

Income tax is a tax on earnings from work and investments. Employers withhold income tax from paychecks. Individuals must file a tax return each year. Tax returns report income and calculate taxes owed. Deductions and credits can reduce tax liability. The Internal Revenue Service (IRS) oversees tax collection. Paying taxes is a civic duty that supports government functions. Late tax payments can result in penalties. Keeping accurate financial records is important for tax filing.

Sales tax is a tax on goods and services purchased. The sales tax rate varies by state and locality. Retailers collect sales tax at the point of sale. The tax is added to the purchase price. Some items, like groceries, may be exempt from sales tax. Sales tax revenue supports public services. Understanding sales tax can help with budgeting. Sales tax is not deductible on federal tax returns. Online purchases may also be subject to sales tax.

Comprehension Questions:

1. What is income tax?

_____

2. What is the role of the IRS?

_____

3. What can happen if one pays taxes late?

_____

4. How is sales tax collected?

_____

5. What supports public services according to the text?

_____

Exercise 8- Read the text aloud before answering the questions.

Medical Services

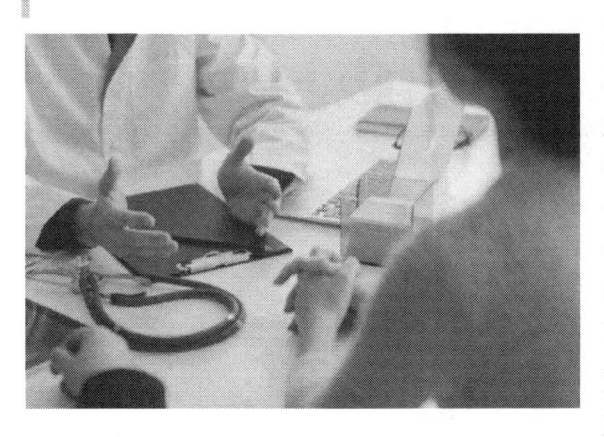

Medical services include a wide range of healthcare options. Primary care doctors provide general health check-ups. Specialists treat specific conditions, like heart disease. Hospitals offer emergency services and surgeries. Clinics provide outpatient care for minor illnesses. Pharmacies dispense medications prescribed by doctors. Preventive care, such as vaccinations, helps prevent infectious diseases. Telemedicine allows patients to consult doctors remotely.

Accessing medical services requires understanding your health insurance plan. Health insurance helps cover the cost of medical services. Plans vary in coverage and cost. It is important to know which services are covered. Some plans require referrals to see specialists. Emergency services are available 24/7. Patients should keep a record of their medical history. Regular check-ups can detect health issues early. Understanding how to use medical services can improve health outcomes. Good communication with healthcare providers is essential.

Comprehension Questions:

1. What are primary care doctors responsible for?
   _____

2. How do specialists differ from primary care doctors?
   _____

3. Why is preventive care important?
   _____

4. What does telemedicine allow patients to do?
   _____

5. Why is it important to understand your health insurance plan?
   _____

Exercise 9- Read the text aloud before answering the questions.

Taking Medication and Dosage

Taking medication correctly is crucial for health. Follow the dosage instructions provided by your doctor. Never share medication with others. Use a pill organizer to keep track of doses. Take medication at the same time each day. Do not skip doses, even if you feel better. Report any side effects to your doctor immediately. Store medication in a cool, dry place. Keep medication out of reach of children.

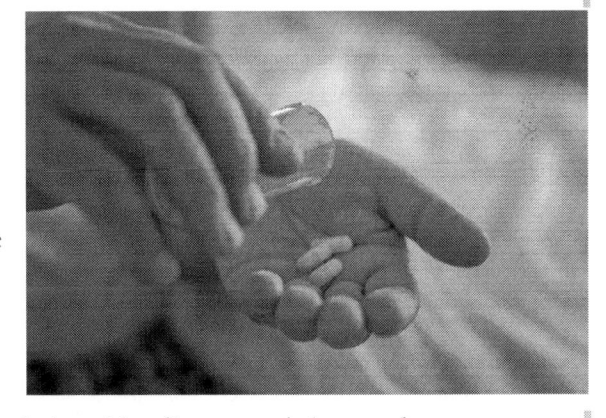

Understanding the purpose of your medication can help with adherence. Ask your doctor or pharmacist about your medication. Read the label and patient information leaflet. Some medications must be taken with food. Others should be taken on an empty stomach. Keep a list of all medications you are taking. Inform your doctor about any other supplements you use. Regularly review your medications with your healthcare provider. Proper medication management improves health outcomes.

Comprehension Questions:

1. Why should you never share medication with others?

_____

2. What is a pill organizer used for?

_____

3. Why is it important to take medication at the same time each day?

_____

4. Where should medication be stored?

_____

5. Why should you inform your doctor about other supplements you use?

_____

Exercise 10- Read the text aloud before answering the questions.

Healthy Habits

Maintaining healthy habits is essential for overall well-being. Eat a balanced diet rich in fruits and vegetables. Exercise regularly to stay fit. Get enough sleep each night. Avoid smoking and limit alcohol consumption. Stay hydrated by drinking plenty of water. Practice good hygiene to prevent illness. Manage stress through relaxation techniques. Regular check-ups with your doctor are important. Healthy habits contribute to a longer, happier life.

Building healthy habits takes time and commitment. Start with small changes and gradually increase. Set realistic goals and track your progress. Find activities you enjoy to stay motivated. Involve friends and family for support. Celebrate your successes and learn from setbacks. Remember that consistency is key. Make healthy living a part of your daily routine. A healthy lifestyle improves both physical and mental health.

Comprehension Questions:

1. What are two components of a balanced diet?

   _____

2. Why is getting enough sleep important?

   _____

3. How can you manage stress?

   _____

4. Why should you involve friends and family in building healthy habits?

   _____

5. What improves both physical and mental health?

   _____

Exercise 11- Read the text aloud before answering the questions.

K-12 School

K-12 education includes kindergarten through 12th grade. Schools provide a structured learning environment. Teachers use lesson plans to educate students. Subjects include math, science, English, and history. Extracurricular activities, like sports and clubs, are also offered. Schools focus on both academic and social development. Parent-teacher conferences help track student progress. Schools have rules and policies to ensure safety. Education is important for future success.

In K-12 schools, students learn essential skills. Reading and writing are fundamental. Math skills are also developed through various levels. Science teaches about the natural world. History provides an understanding of the past. Physical education promotes fitness and health. Arts and music encourage creativity. Schools prepare students for higher education and careers. A supportive school environment enhances learning.

Comprehension Questions:

1. What grades are included in K-12 education?

   _____

2. Name two subjects taught in K-12 schools.

   _____

3. Why are parent-teacher conferences important?

   _____

4. What does physical education promote?

   _____

5. How do schools prepare students for the future?

   _____

Exercise 12- Read the text aloud before answering the questions.

Housing and Rent

Finding suitable housing is important for a stable life. Renting is a common option for many people. Apartments and houses are available for rent. Rent prices vary based on location and size. It is important to sign a lease agreement. The lease outlines the terms and conditions of renting. Renters should understand their rights and responsibilities. Paying rent on time is crucial. Maintenance requests should be reported to the landlord.

Saving for a home purchase is another option. Homeownership provides stability and investment opportunities. A mortgage is needed to buy a home. It is important to budget for homeownership expenses. Property taxes, insurance, and maintenance costs should be considered. Home inspections are essential before purchasing. Home equity can be built over time. Understanding the housing market is important. Both renting and owning have their pros and cons.

Comprehension Questions:

1. What is a lease agreement?

   _____

2. Why is it important to pay rent on time?

   _____

3. What are two expenses to budget for in homeownership?

   _____

4. Why are home inspections important before purchasing?

   _____

5. What can be built over time in homeownership?

   _____

Exercise 13- Read the text aloud before answering the questions.

Career and Technical Education Classes

Career and technical education (CTE) classes prepare students for specific careers. Courses include hands-on training and practical skills. Subjects range from healthcare to technology. Students can earn certifications in their fields. CTE programs often partner with local businesses. Internships provide real-world experience, so graduates are ready to enter the workforce. CTE classes offer an alternative to traditional academic paths. They focus on career readiness and skill development.

CTE programs are available in high schools and colleges. They help meet the demand for skilled workers. Students learn industry-specific knowledge. These classes often have smaller class sizes and instructors are usually industry professionals. Programs can lead to high-paying jobs. Financial aid may be available for CTE students. Continuous learning is encouraged in technical fields. CTE education supports economic growth and development.

Comprehension Questions:

1. What do CTE classes prepare students for?

   _____

2. How do CTE programs provide real-world experience?

   _____

3. How are CTE classes different from traditional academic paths?

   _____

4. What is a benefit of smaller class sizes in CTE programs?

   _____

5. How does CTE education support economic growth?

   _____

Answer Keys

Exercise 1- Workplace Safety Procedures

1. Helmets, gloves, and safety glasses are mentioned.
2. Fire drills are conducted monthly.
3. Clear communication is important to maintain a safe environment.
4. Employees should know the location of fire extinguishers and first aid kits.

Exercise 2- Types of Transportation

1. Public transportation reduces traffic congestion, pollution, and is cost-effective.
2. Bicycles and electric vehicles are two forms of eco-friendly transportation.
3. It might be considered expensive due to fuel and maintenance costs.
4. Carpooling reduces expenses and environmental impact.

3. Preventative care prevents infectious diseases.
4. It allows patients to consult with doctors remotely.
5. It is important so you know the services covered and the costs.

Exercise 9- Taking Medication and Dosage

1. It may affect them differently and harm them.
2. A pill organizer is used to keep track of doses.
3. It is important to maintain a routine and ensure a consistent amount of medication is in your body.
4. Medication should be stored in a cool, dry place.
5. You should tell your doctor to avoid any interactions between the medication and supplements.

Exercise 3- Managing a House Budget

1. Listing all sources of income is the first step.
2. Savings is important for financial stability and emergencies.
3. Meal planning reduces grocery costs.
4. The family should be involved as a well-managed budget leads to financial security.
5. Energy-efficient appliances lower utility bills.

Exercise 4- Elections in the US

1. The process begins with primary elections.
2. Registration is important to ensure citizens can cast their vote.
3. Elections are held at local, state, and national levels.
4. Citizens can vote in person or by mail.
5. The peaceful transfer of power is a hallmark of democracy.

Exercise 5- Voting in the US

1. Citizens over the age of 18 are eligible to vote.
2. Citizens can register online or in person.
3. Campaigns provide information through advertisements and debates.
4. Identification may be required to vote.
5. Participation in elections strengthens democracy.

Exercise 6- Looking for Jobs

1. You should update your resume.
2. Networking helps you learn about job opportunities.

Exercise 10- Healthy Habits

1. Fruits and vegetables are two components of a balanced diet.
2. Enough sleep is important for overall well-being.
3. You can manage stress through relaxation techniques.
4. You should involve them for support and motivation.
5. A healthy lifestyle improves both physical and mental health.

Exercise 11- K-12 School

1. It includes kindergarten through 12th grade.
2. Math and science are two subjects taught.
   (Answer may also include English, history, physical education and arts and music.)
3. Parent-teacher conferences help track student progress.
4. Physical education promotes fitness and health.
5. Schools prepare students for higher education and careers.

Exercise 12- Housing and Rent

1. It is a document outlining the terms and conditions of renting.
2. Paying rent on time is important to avoid penalties and maintain good standing.
3. Two expenses are property taxes and insurance.
4. Inspections ensure the property is in good condition.
5. Home equity can be built over time.

3. You can prepare for interviews by practicing common questions.
4. You should send a thank-you note.
5. Job search websites and job alerts are mentioned in the text.

Exercise 7- Income and Sales Taxes

1. Income tax is a tax on earnings from work and investments.
2. The IRS oversees tax collection.
3. Late tax payments can result in penalties.
4. Sales tax is collected at the point of sale by retailers.
5. Sales tax revenue supports public services.

Exercise 8- Medical Services

1. Primary care doctors are responsible for general health check-ups.
2. They treat specific conditions.

Exercise 13- Career and Technical Education Classes

1. They prepare students for specific careers.
2. They provide real-world experiences through internships.
3. They focus on career readiness and practical skills.
4. Smaller class sizes offer more personalized instruction.
5. It meets the demand for skilled workers.

REFLECTION ON LEARNING

Let's reflect on your progress.

1. What sounds did you learn and practice?

2. What sounds do you struggle with?

3. What strategies can you use to make more progress?

4. What do you want your instructor to know about your challenges?

LESSON 10

STRATEGIES TO INCREASE YOUR VOCABULARY AND IMPROVE YOUR READING SKILLS

Vocabulary Building Strategies

Follow the strategies below to increase your vocabulary.

	Actions
1	Read every day.
2	Use a dictionary.
3	Learn new words weekly.
4	Write new words in a notebook.
5	Use flashcards to review words.
6	Play word games.
7	Join a book club.

8	Watch educational videos.
9	Talk with friends in English.
10	Practice using new words in sentences.

Reading Strategies

Follow the strategies below to develop and improve your reading comprehension skills.

	Strategies
1	Read every day.
2	Read difficult texts slowly and carefully.
3	Highlight or underline main ideas and highlight key details.
4	Take notes while reading.
5	Summarize each paragraph in your own words.
6	Discuss what you read with others.
7	Ask questions about the text.
8	Make predictions about what will happen next.
9	Visualize the scenes in your mind.
10	Connect the text to your own experiences.

ABOUT CBL

Coaching for Better Learning (CBL) helps adult education and workforce service providers improve and create professional development and instructional systems to maximize student engagement, retention—and learning.

CBL takes pride in publishing learner-centered student textbooks designed to prepare learners for standardized assessments (CASAS, TABE 11&12, HiSET, and GED) and to assist instructors in covering course curricula and standards— aligned with NRS, ELPS, and WIOA expectations—with confidence.

Our publications also include teaching guides, test prep tools, and study guides that foster reflective learning, ensuring sustained engagement in active learning. Find our meticulously crafted textbooks on our book page (cbledu.com) or major platforms like Amazon, Barnes & Noble, and Ingram Spark.

CBL also guides adult education and workforce programs in establishing robust professional development programs—training, peer-mentoring, coaching, community of practices (CoPs), and instructional systems— fostering a culture of continuous improvement and contributing to higher learner retention and success rates.

Additionally, we offer workshops and PD sessions for adult educators and classroom instructors. We design and implement our sessions using robust and evidence-based frameworks (Bloom Taxonomy, brain-based learning, systems thinking) and adult learning theories (Transformational Learning, Andragogy, Theory of Margin, and Self-Directed learning).

Our diverse solutions are intricately designed to enrich students' learning experiences and simplify instructors' jobs. Examples of our professional development solutions include:

1. High-impact teaching practices.
2. Promoting high-impact student retention practices.
3. Giving clear and effective instructions.
4. Digital literacy that focuses on learning.
5. Reflective teaching practices to maximize learning.
6. Learning theories and frameworks for high-impact instructions.
7. Leveraging instructional technology (TPACK: Technological, Pedagogical, and Content Knowledge) for high-impact teaching.
8. Applying evidence-based strategies for engaging learners and maximizing their performance on standardized testing.

If you have questions about instructional systems, textbooks, or student learning and retention, contact us today at teamcbl@cbledu.com or 410-960-4082.

MORE TEXTBOOKS BY CBL

ADULT ED MATH
NUMBER SYSTEM, NUMBER SENSE, AND OPERATIONS PREPARING
FOR
CASAS, TABE 11 & 12, HISET, AND GED TESTING
BY COACHING FOR BETTER LEARNING
ADULT ED MATH
GEOMETRY PREPARING
FOR
CASAS, TABE 11 & 12, HISET, AND GED TESTING
BY COACHING FOR BETTER LEARNING
CBL COACHING FOR BETTER LEARNING
Math
Practice Worksheets and Workbook for Adult Students
SKILLS FOR SUCCESS IN CAREER AND TECHNICAL EDUCATION (CTE)
STUDENT GUIDE
A SYSTEMATIC WAY TO MASTER ORGANIZATIONAL AND SOFT SKILLS
CBL COACHING
BY COACHING FOR BETTER LEARNING, LLC
cbledu.com
HOW TO ACHIEVE BETTER STUDENT RETENTION IN ADULT EDUCATION
TEDDY EDOUARD
TABE 11 & 12 CONSUMABLE STUDENT READING MANUAL FOR LEVEL E
By Coaching for Better Learning, LLC
TABE 11 & 12 CONSUMABLE STUDENT READING MANUAL FOR LEVEL M
By Coaching for Better Learning, LLC
TABE 11 & 12 CONSUMABLE STUDENT READING MANUAL FOR LEVEL D
By Coaching for Better Learning, LLC
TABE 11 & 12 STUDENT LANGUAGE MANUAL FOR LEVEL E
By Coaching for Better Learning, LLC
TABE 11 & 12 STUDENT LANGUAGE MANUAL FOR LEVEL M
By Coaching for Better Learning, LLC
TABE 11 & 12 Consumable Student Math Workbook FOR LEVEL E
Preparing Adult Learners for TABE 11 & 12 Math Tests and for Vocational Training Entrance Math Exams
By Coaching for Better Learning, LLC
TABE 11 & 12 Consumable Student Math Workbook FOR LEVEL M
Preparing Adult Learners for TABE 11 & 12 Math Tests and for Vocational Training Entrance Math Exams
By Coaching for Better Learning, LLC
TABE 11 & 12 Consumable Student Math Workbook FOR LEVEL D
Preparing Adult Learners for TABE 11 & 12 Math Tests and for Vocational Training Entrance Math Exams
By Coaching for Better Learning, LLC
TABE 11 & 12 Consumable Student Math Workbook FOR LEVEL A
Preparing Adult Learners for TABE 11 & 12 Math Tests and for Vocational Training Entrance Math Exams
By Coaching for Better Learning, LLC
READING NOTEBOOK & JOURNAL
For Adult Students
By Coaching For Better Learning
MATH NOTEBOOK & JOURNAL
For Adult Students
By Coaching For Better Learning
CBL COACHING FOR BETTER LEARNING
Workbook
Number and Letter Tracing for Adult Students
This tool is designed to help adult students practice and master handwriting. It is appropriate for literacy, ESL, and ABE classes.
BOOK 1
PHONICS AND LIFE SKILLS READING FOR Adult Literacy, ABE, and ESL Students
Turning Learners into Proficient Readers
CBL COACHING FOR BETTER LEARNING

Made in the USA
Monee, IL
18 April 2025